1000 BIG WORDS
for Little Experts

First published in 2025 by Miles Kelly Publishing Ltd
Harding's Barn, Bardfield End Green, Thaxted, Essex, CM6 3PX, UK
Unit 5A The Court, Ashbourne Industrial Estate, Ashbourne,
Co. Meath, A84 DP73, Eire

Copyright © Miles Kelly Publishing Ltd 2025

2 4 6 8 10 9 7 5 3 1

Publishing Director Fran Bromage

Creative Director Jo Cowan

Senior Editors Ruth Redford, Becky Miles

Designers Joanna Lambert, Sam South

Production Elizabeth Collins

Reprographics Stephan Davis

Concept by Fran Bromage
Written by Camilla de la Bédoyère and Fran Bromage
Consulted by Emma Ranade and Camilla de la Bédoyère
All artwork is from the Miles Kelly Artwork Bank

All rights reserved. No part of this publication may be reproduced, stored in a retrieval system, or transmitted by any means, electronic, mechanical, photocopying, recording or otherwise, without the prior permission of the copyright holder.

ISBN 978-1-83515-091-7

Printed in China

British Library Cataloguing-in-Publication Data
A catalogue record for this book is available from the British Library

Made with paper from a sustainable forest

www.mileskelly.net

1000 BiG WORDS
for Little Experts

Miles Kelly

Contents

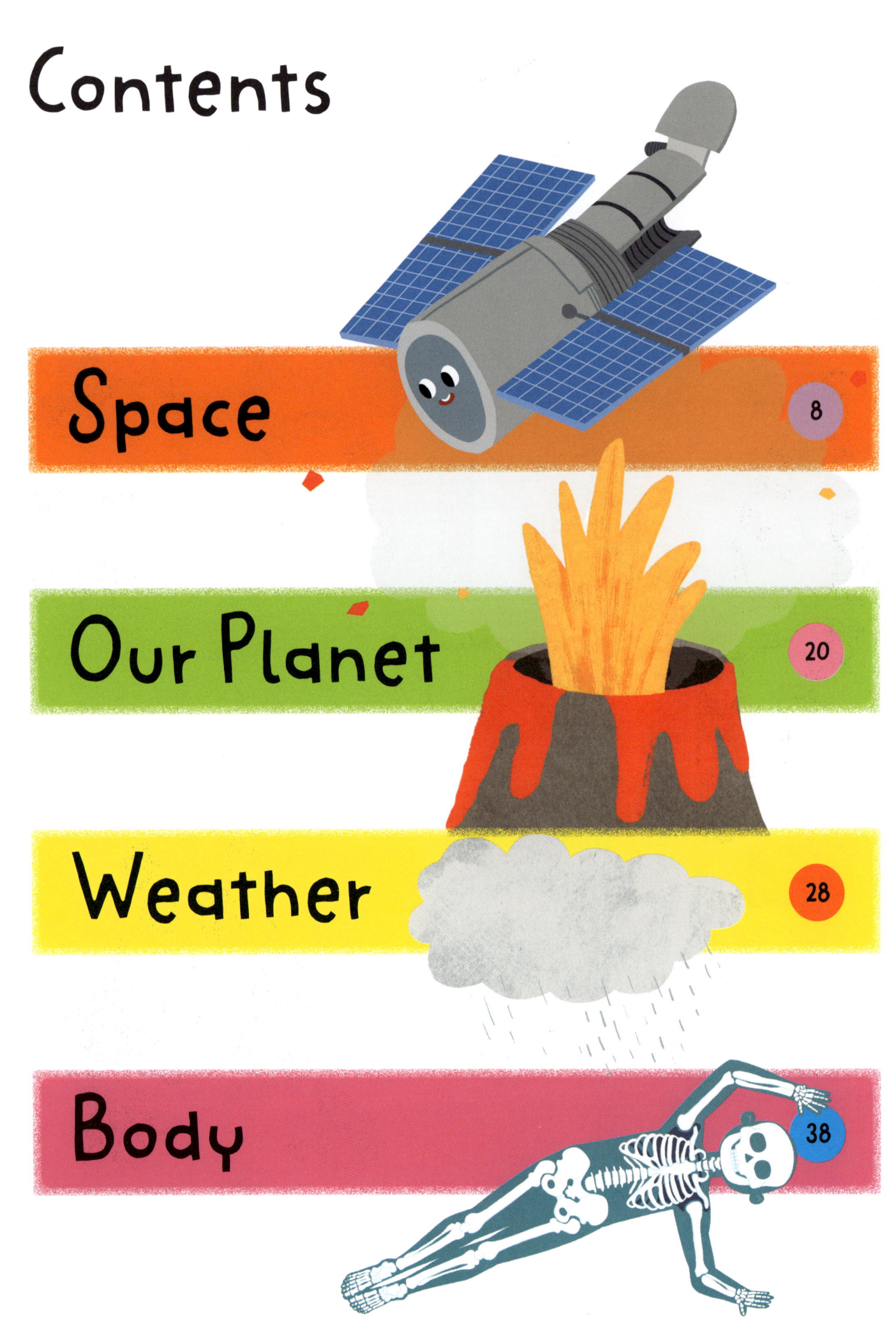

Space	8
Our Planet	20
Weather	28
Body	38

Habitats 52

Animals 86

Birds 102

Bugs 116

Dinosaurs 130

Space

Our Solar System is part of a huge galaxy called the **Milky Way**, which contains at least 100 billion stars.

Universe

barred spiral galaxy

dust and gas clouds

There are eight **planets** that orbit a star called the Sun in our Solar System.

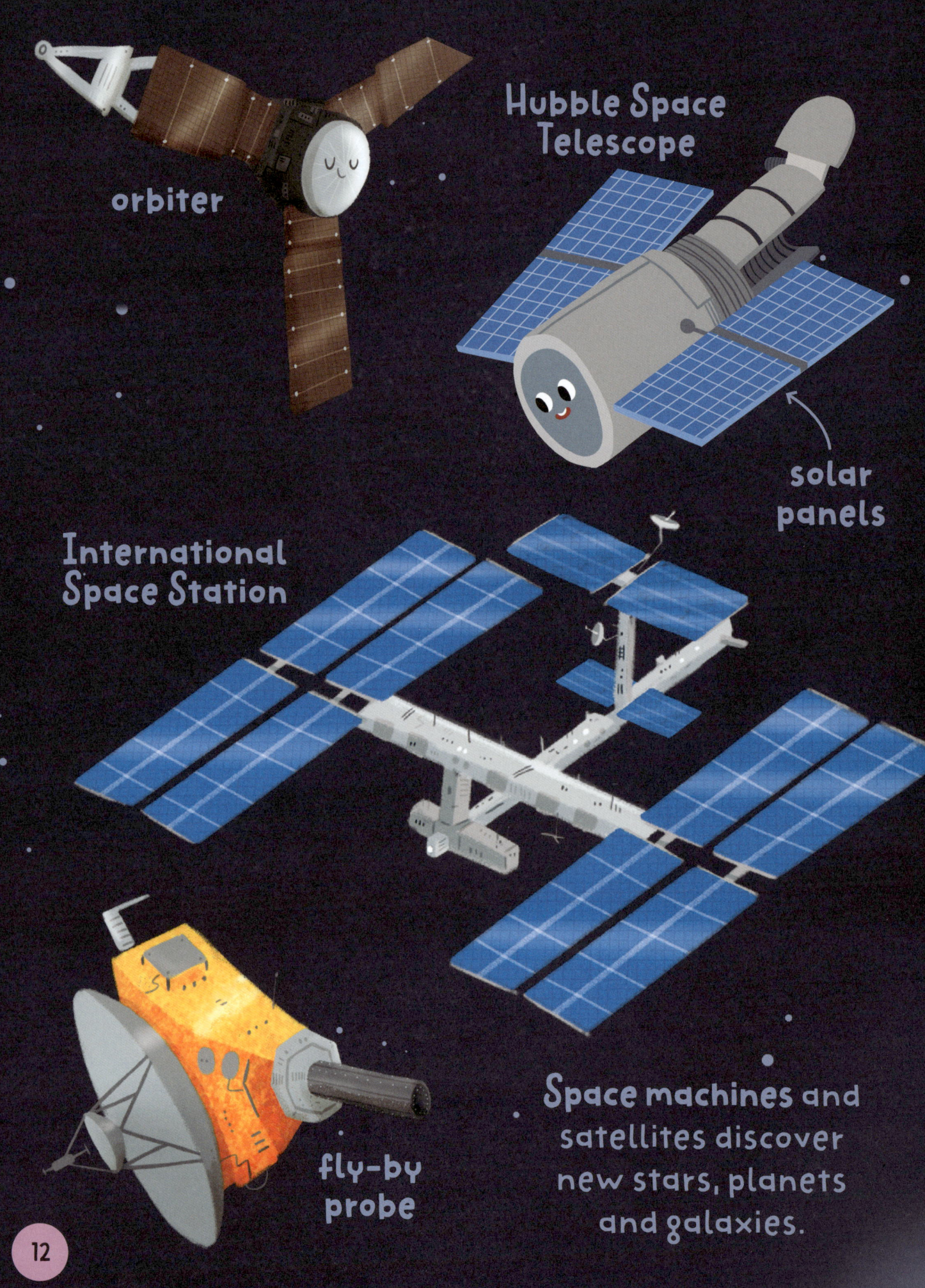

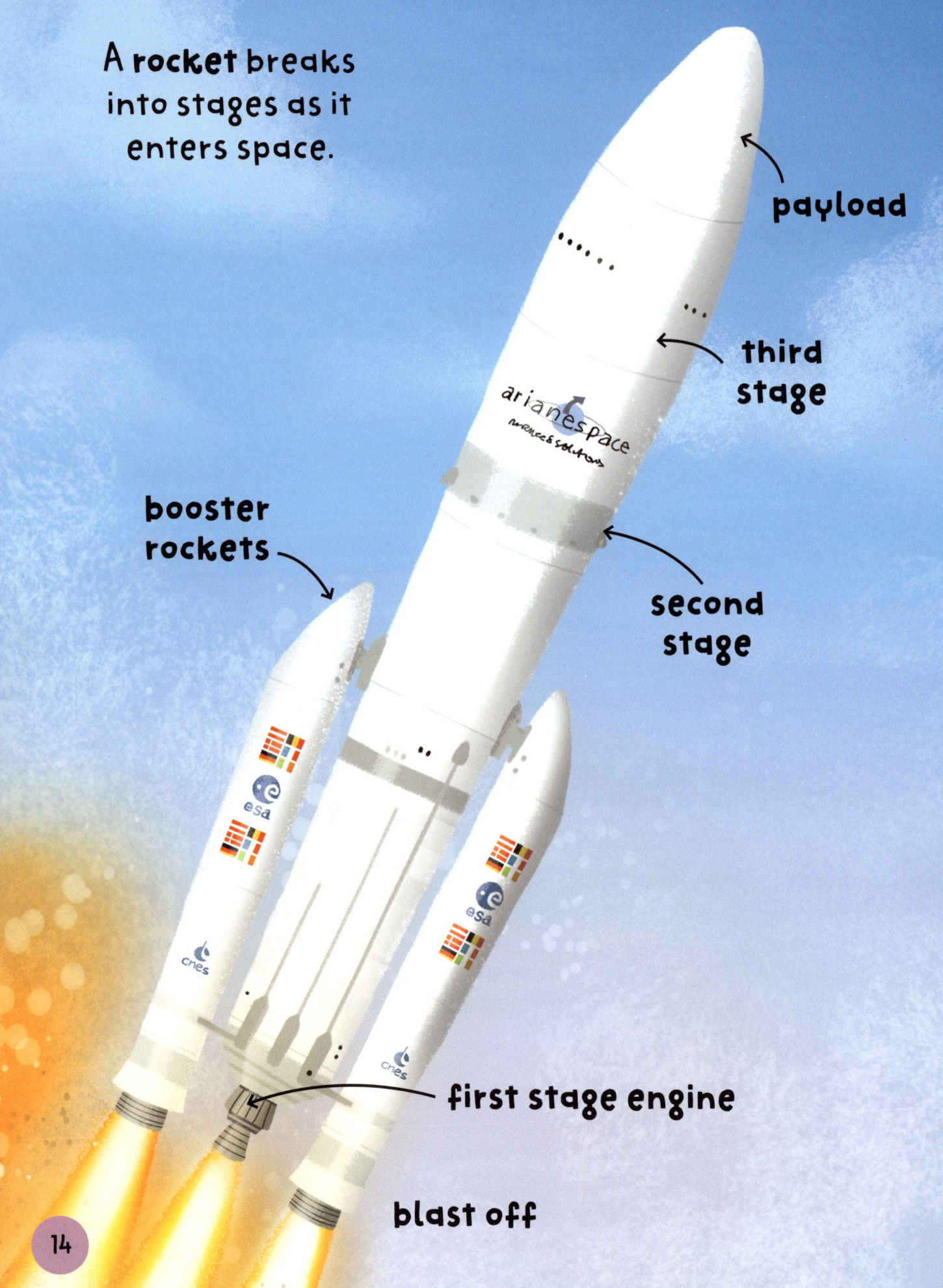

Astronauts go on spacewalks when they visit a space station.

- helmet
- life support pack
- padded gloves
- tether to spacecraft
- protective space suit
- space boots

corona

convection zone

The **Sun** is a very hot star. It gives us **light** and **heat**, which are types of **energy**.

core

sun spot

radiative zone

photosphere

chromosphere

There are billions of **stars** in the Universe. They are all different colours and sizes.

blue super giant

red giant

red dwarf

yellow dwarf

solar flare

Some stars end their lives in huge explosions. These are called supernovas.

supernova

lunar module

astronaut

footprints

extravehicular mobility unit suit

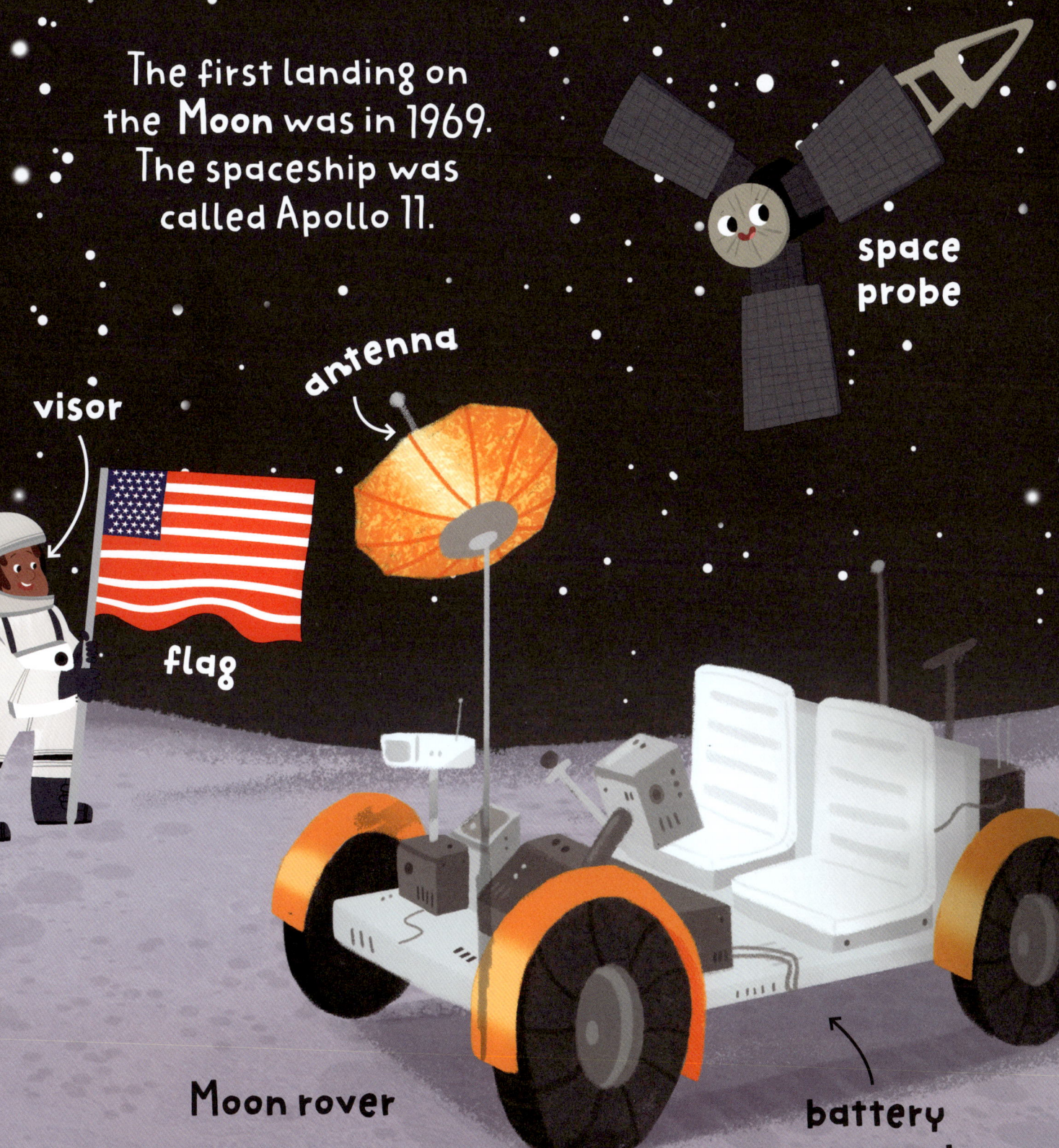

Our Planet

Earth's **surface** is like a jigsaw — made up of lots of rocky pieces called **plates** that fit together.

molten rock

ash cloud

crater

tectonic plates

lava flow

erupting volcano

crust

mantle

Our planet has seven **continents**. The **Equator** is an imaginary line that cuts the Earth in two halves.

Areas of the world can be divided into **climates**. They have regular weather patterns within each region.

Some parts of our planet are very **cold**...

snow

snowflakes

ice sheet

polar bear

ice floe

There are five **oceans** on our planet. They join together to make one huge World Ocean teeming with life.

rock pool

starfish

seahorse

coral

shoal

blue parrotfish

rocky reef

Weather

As Earth moves around the Sun, the two different **hemispheres** get different **seasons**.

northern hemisphere

direction of orbit

North Pole

atmosphere

air currents

Earth

South Pole

Weather happens high up in the sky — in a layer of gases called the **atmosphere**.

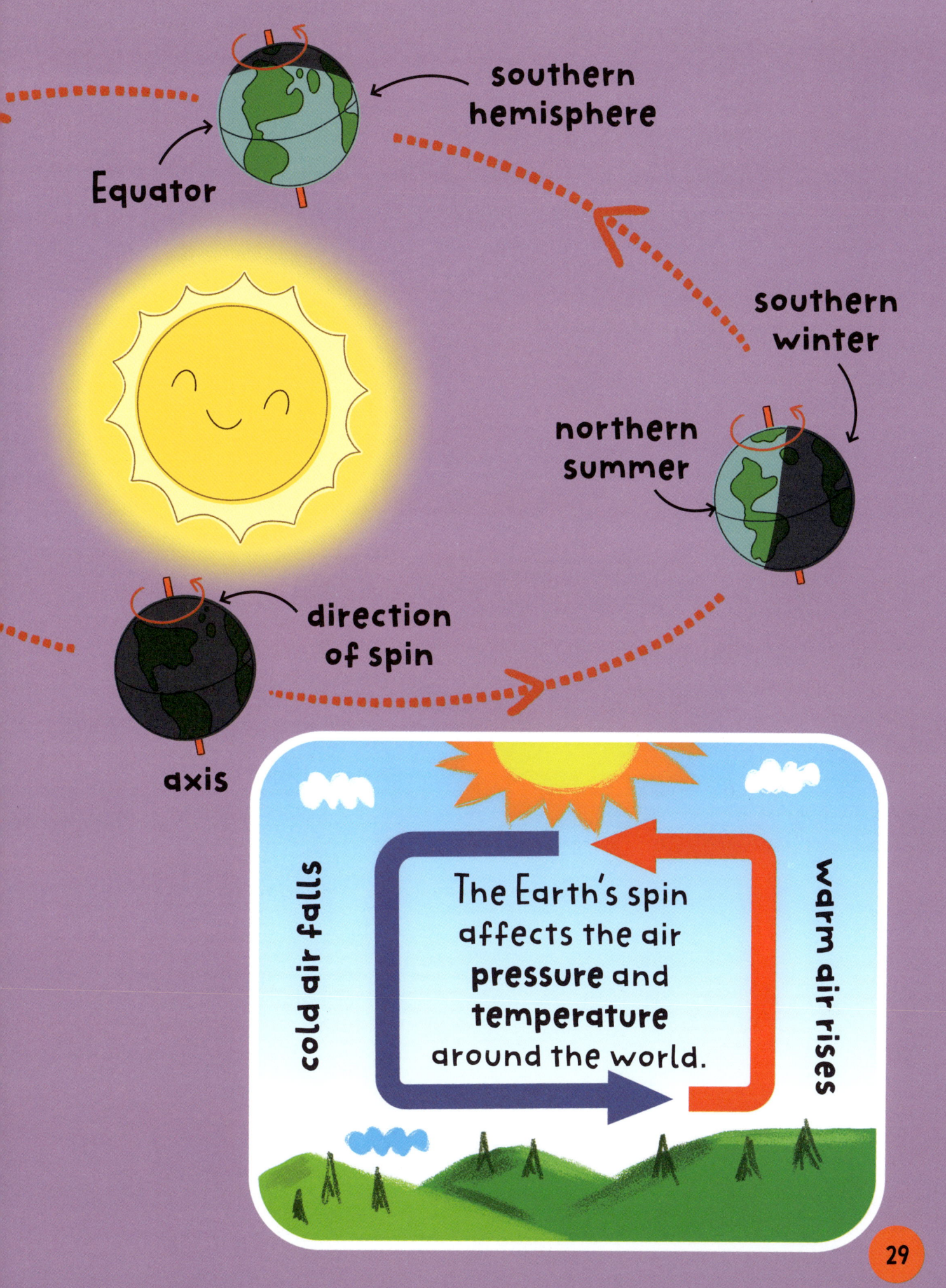

Water is all around us. It moves endlessly from land to sea to air as a **water cycle** to help create our weather.

Sun's heat

clouds form

evaporation

water vapour

sea

salt water

weather symbols

 sun

 rain

 snow

 stormy

 cloudy

 mixed

 foggy

 wind

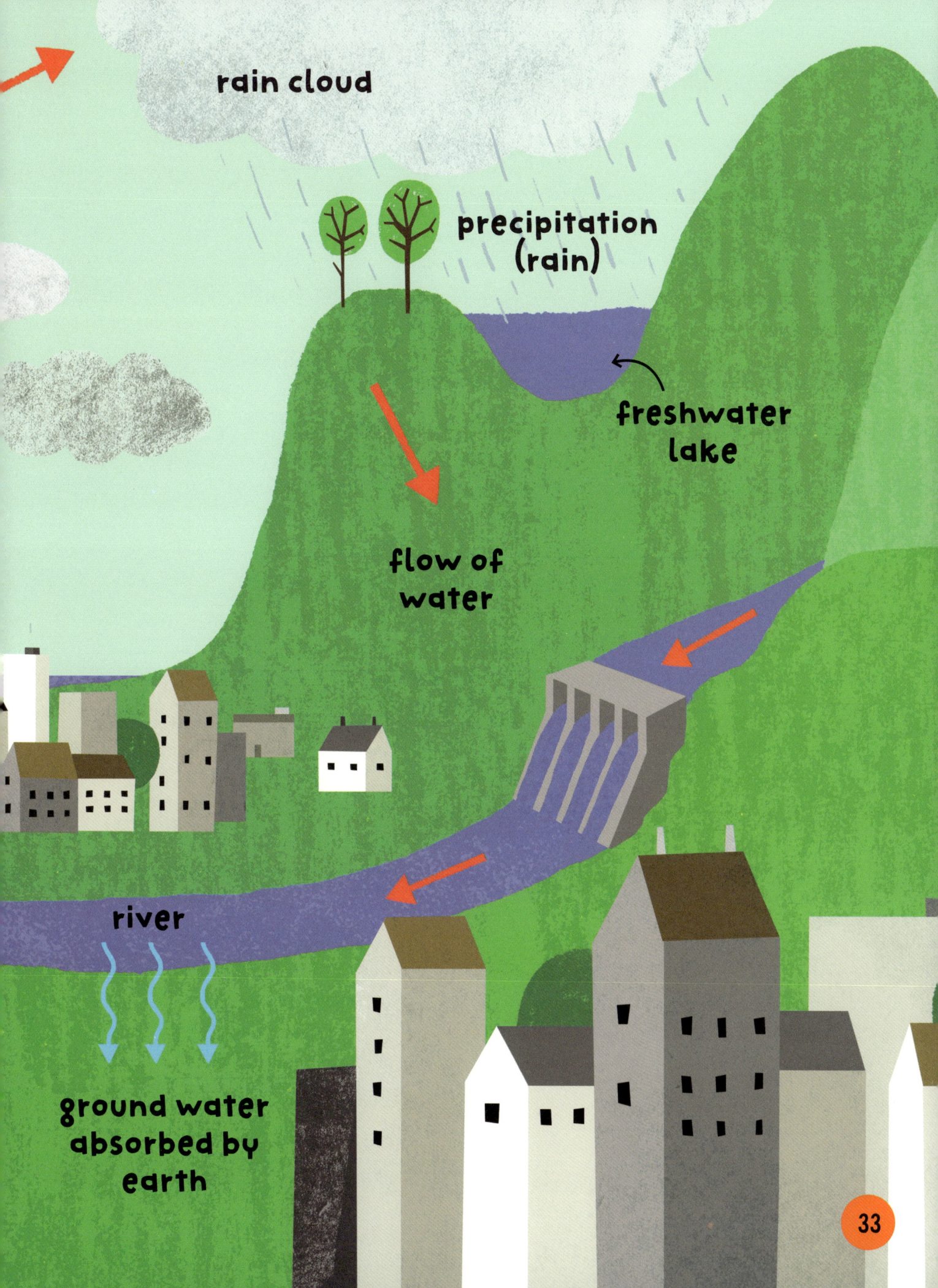

cirrocumulus

cirrostratus

altostratus

altocumulus

stratocumulus

stratus

Clouds are made of tiny water **droplets** or **ice crystals**. The shapes they make all have different names.

35

Rainbows are made when sunlight passes through rain or mist.

Body

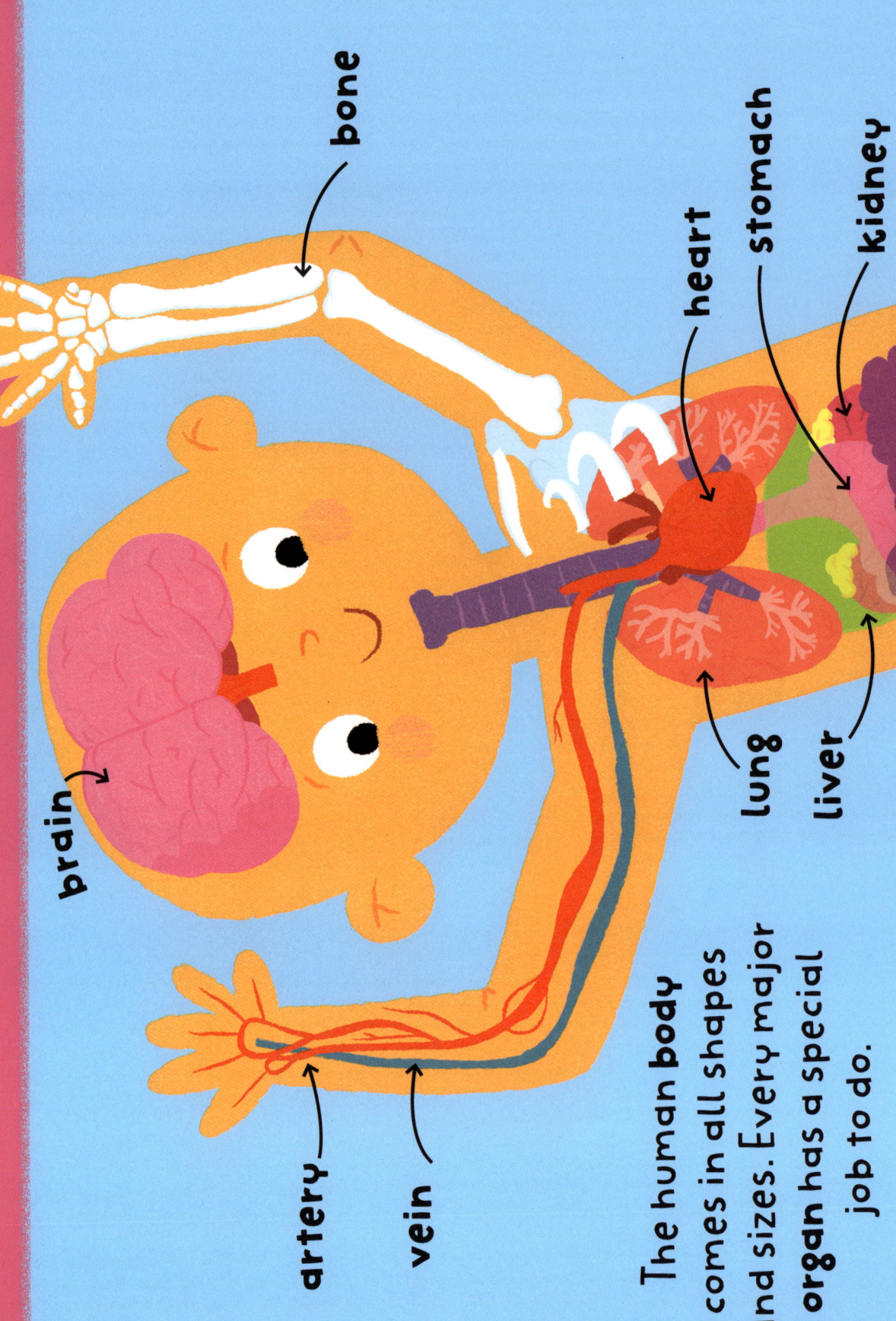

- bone
- heart
- stomach
- kidney
- lung
- liver
- brain
- artery
- vein

The human **body** comes in all shapes and sizes. Every major **organ** has a special job to do.

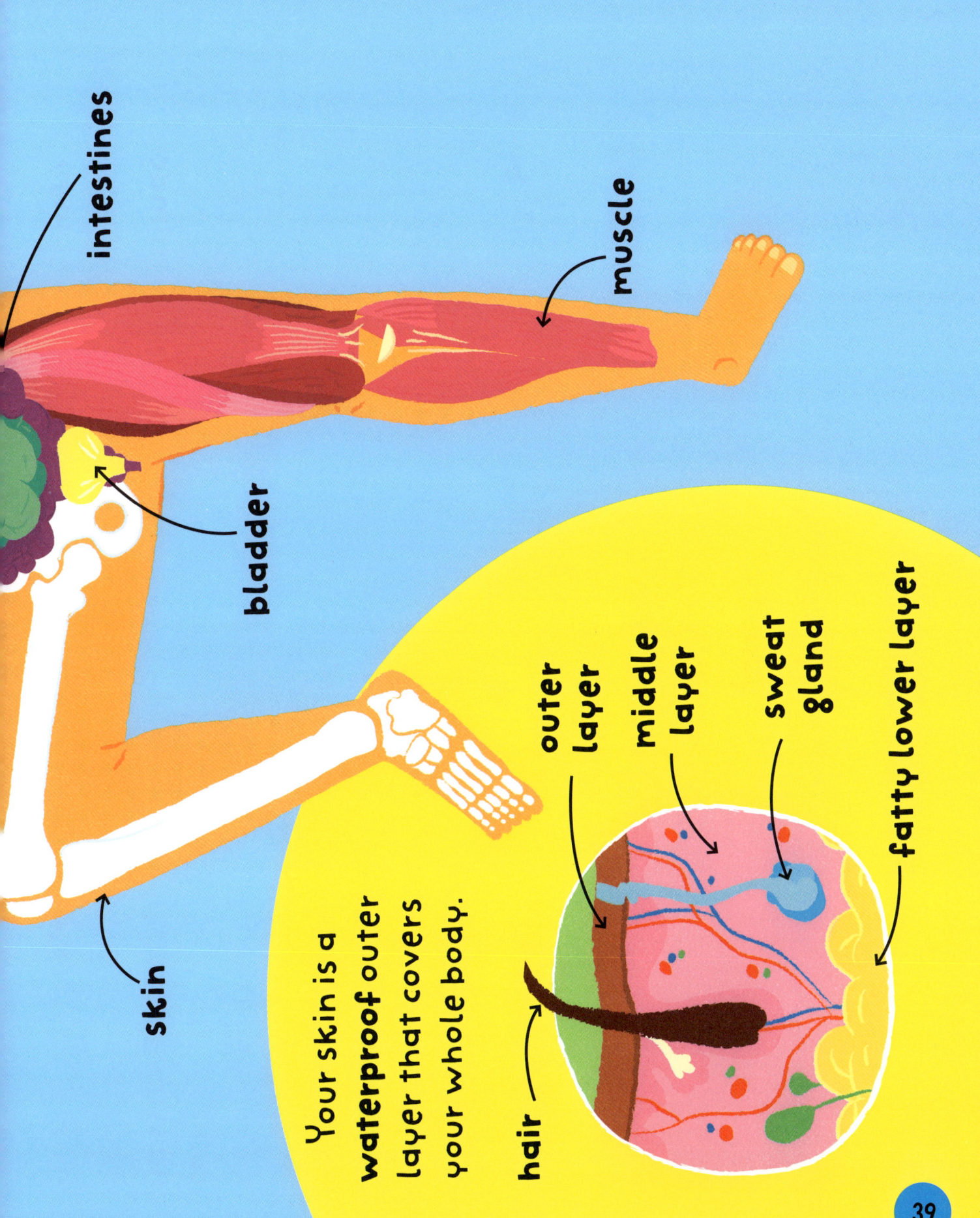

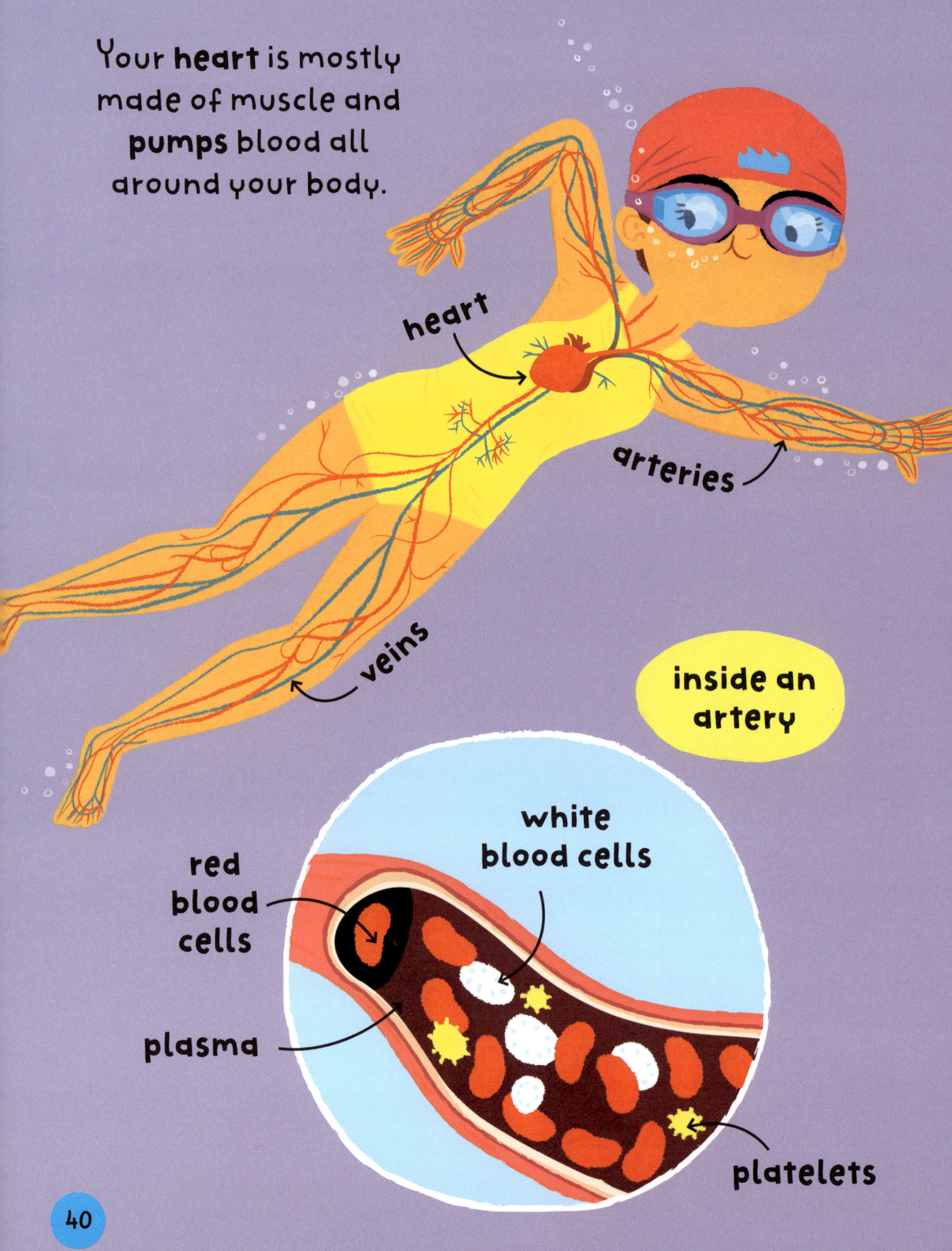

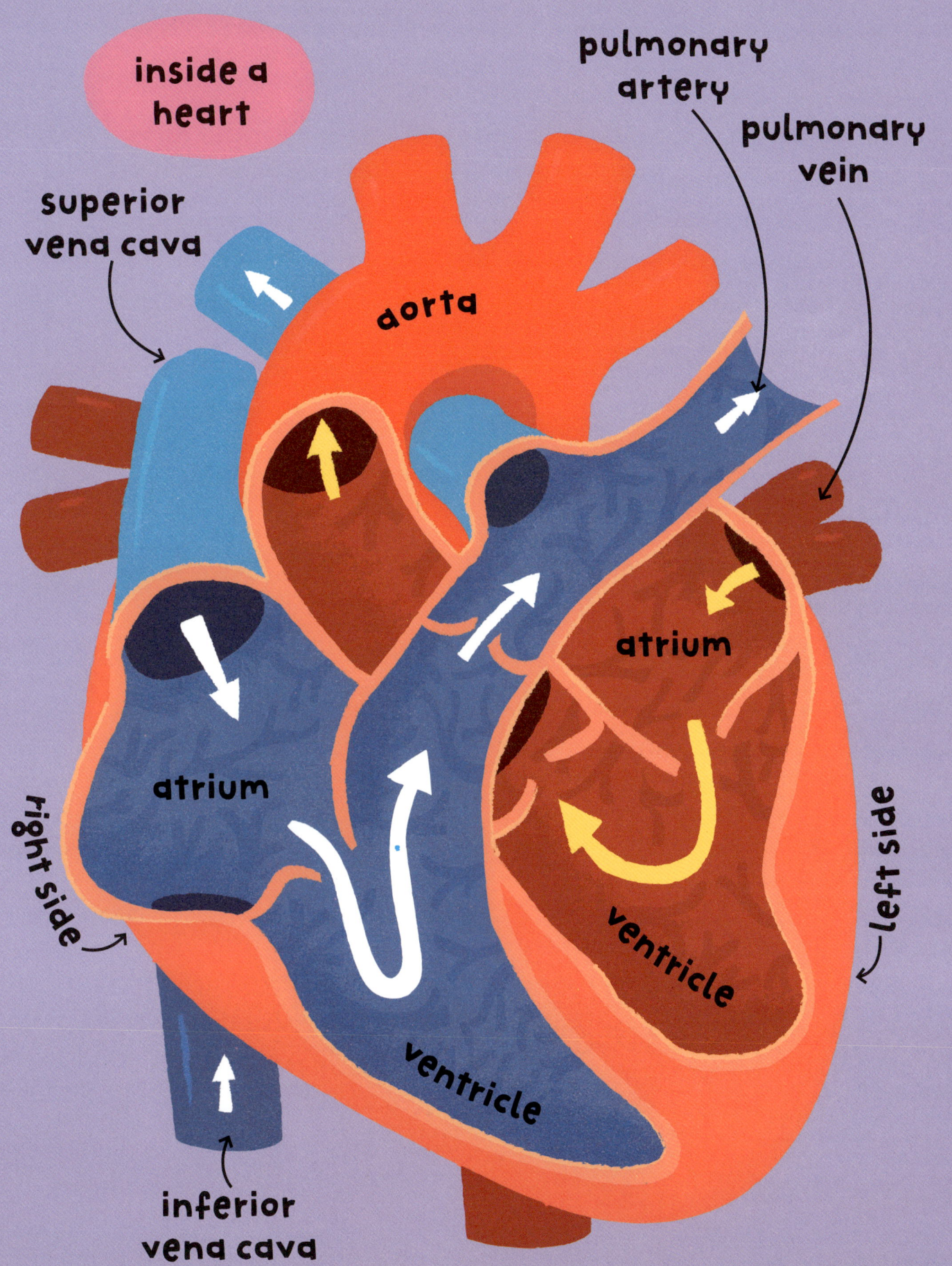

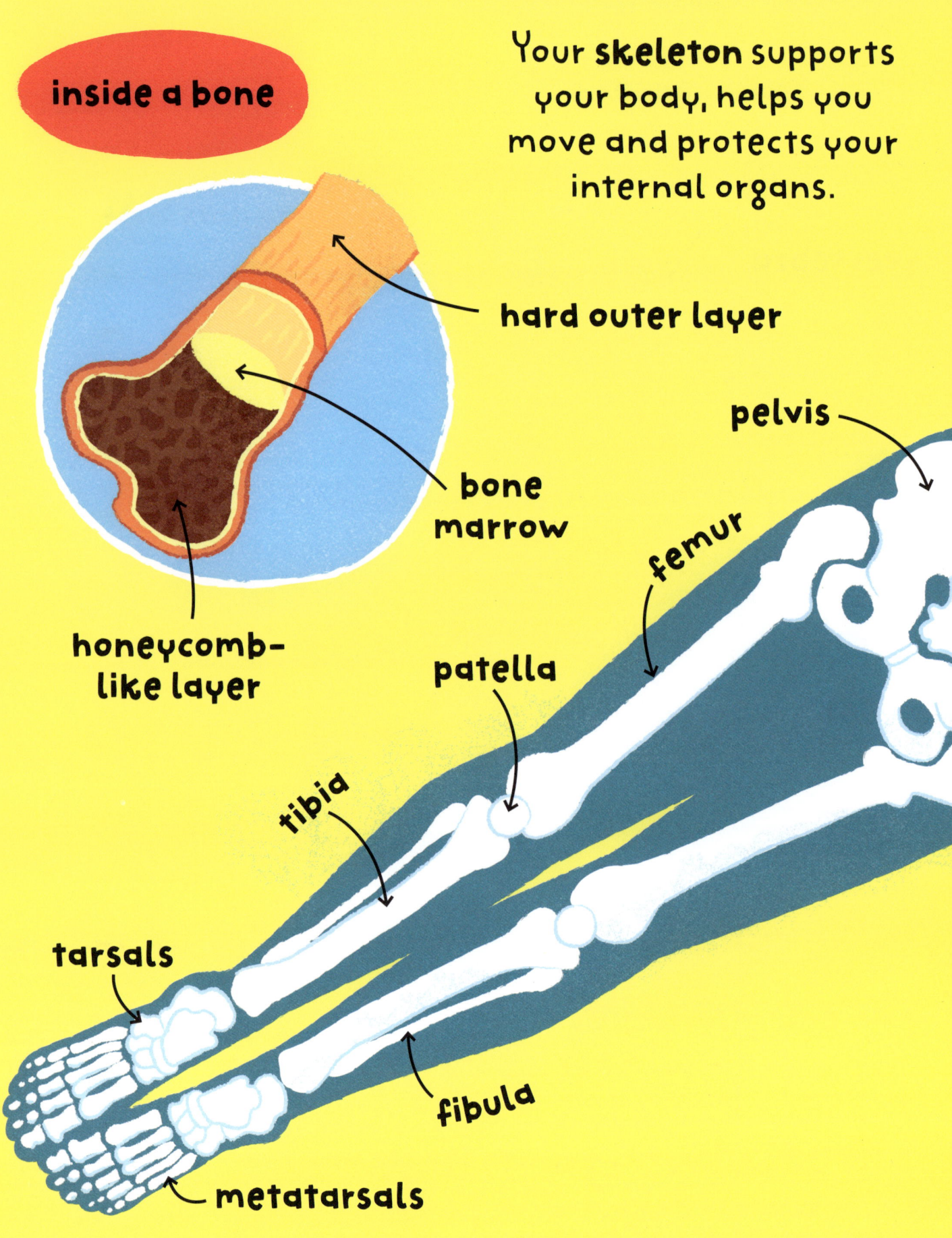

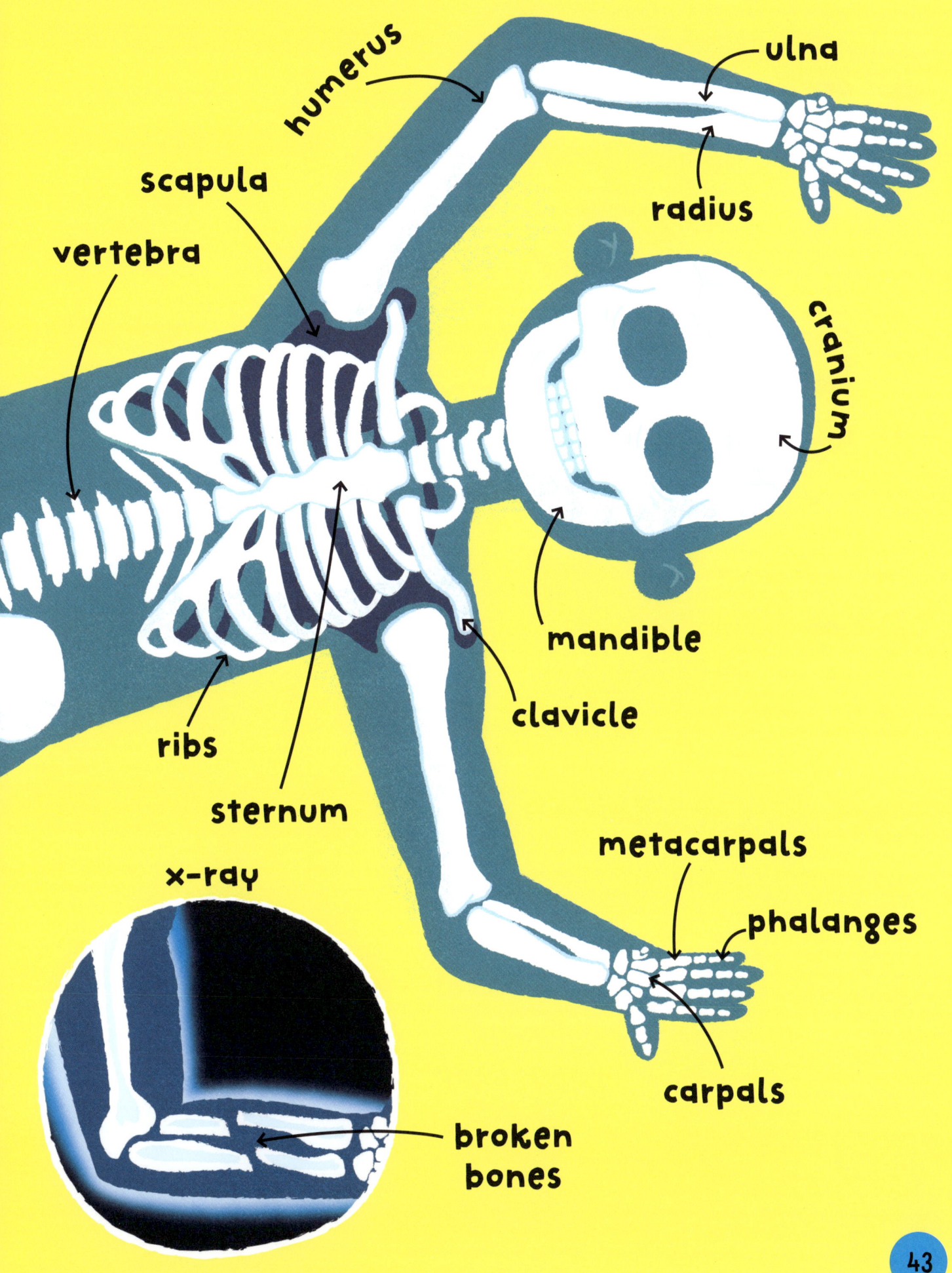

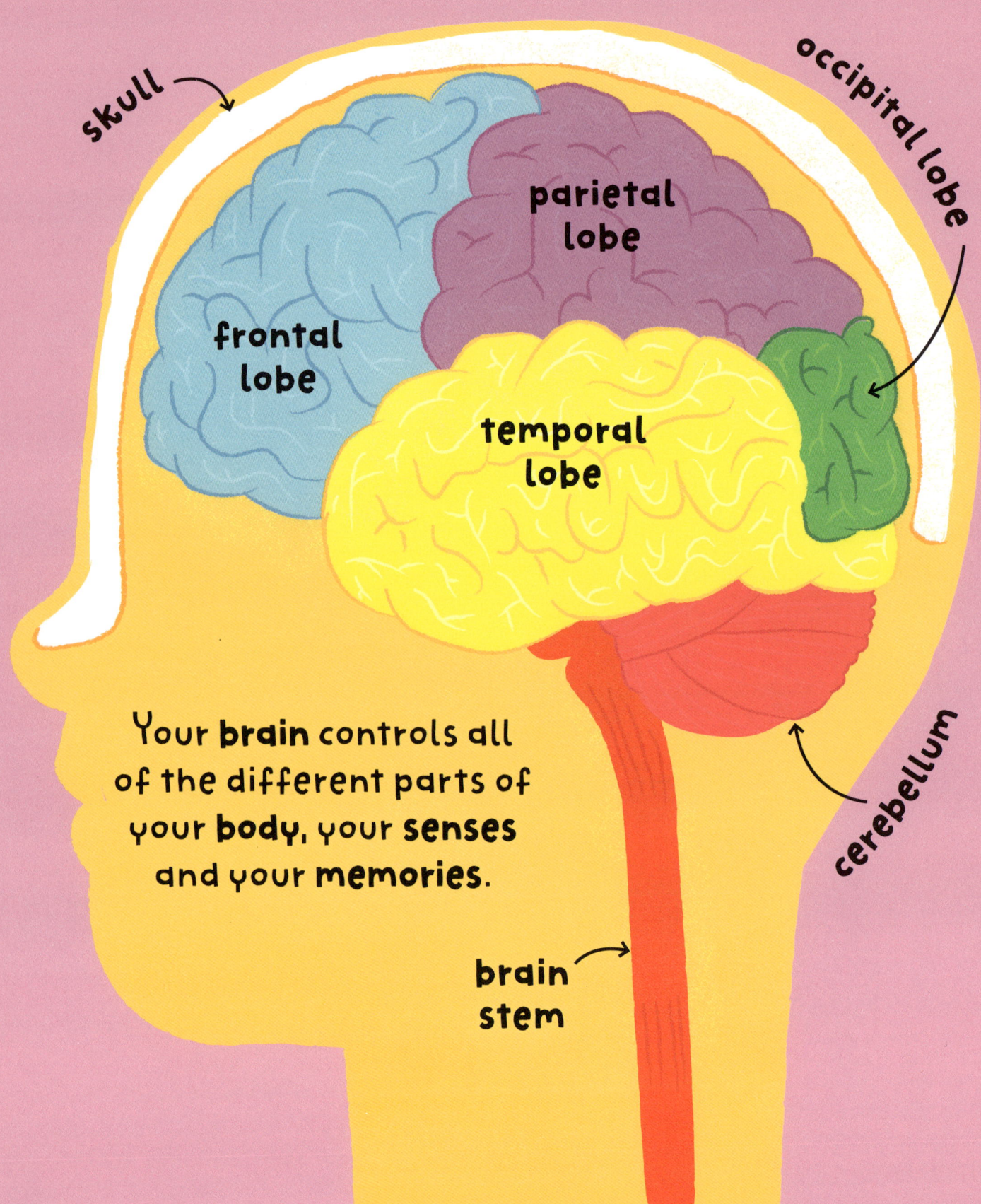

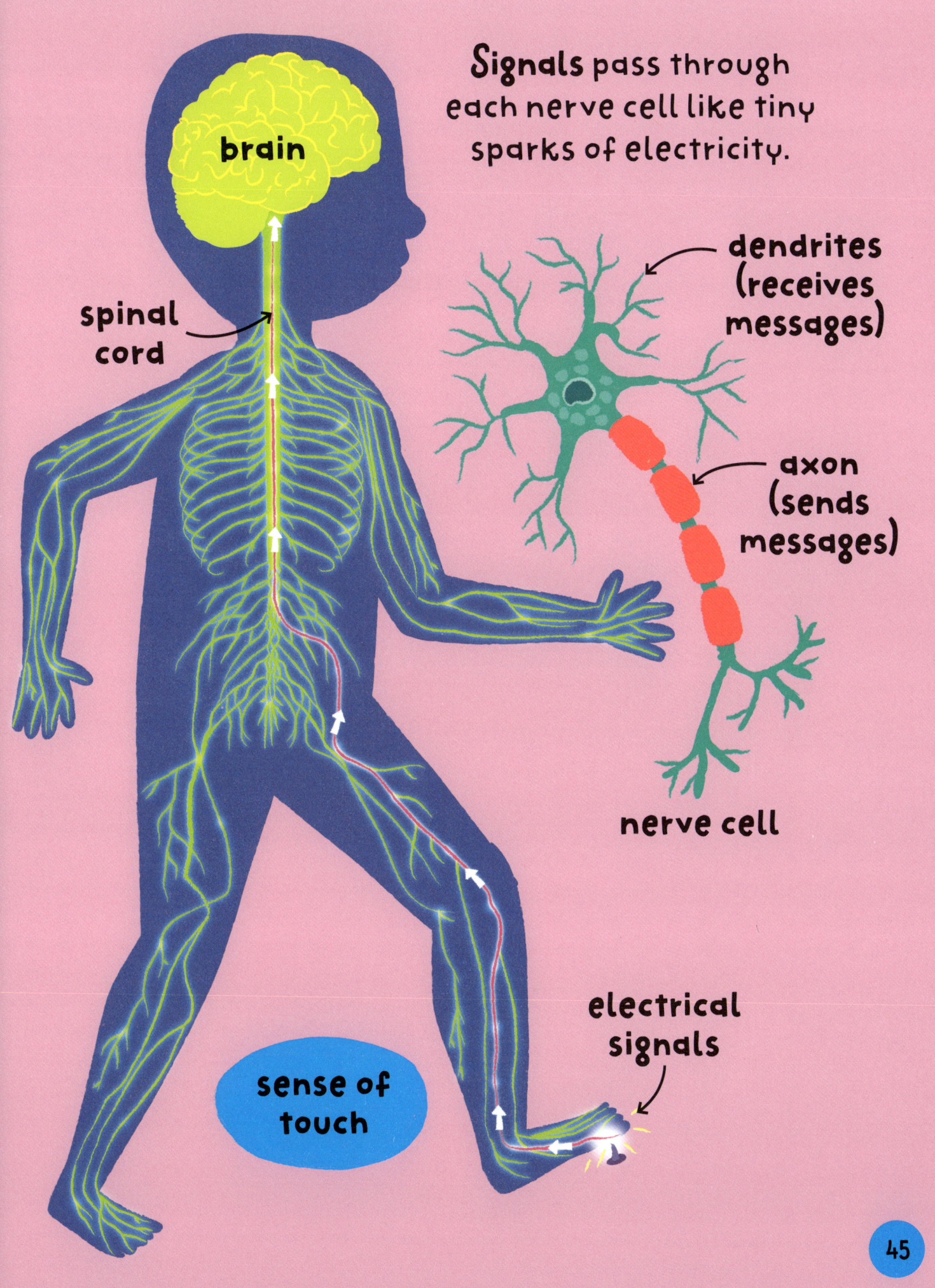

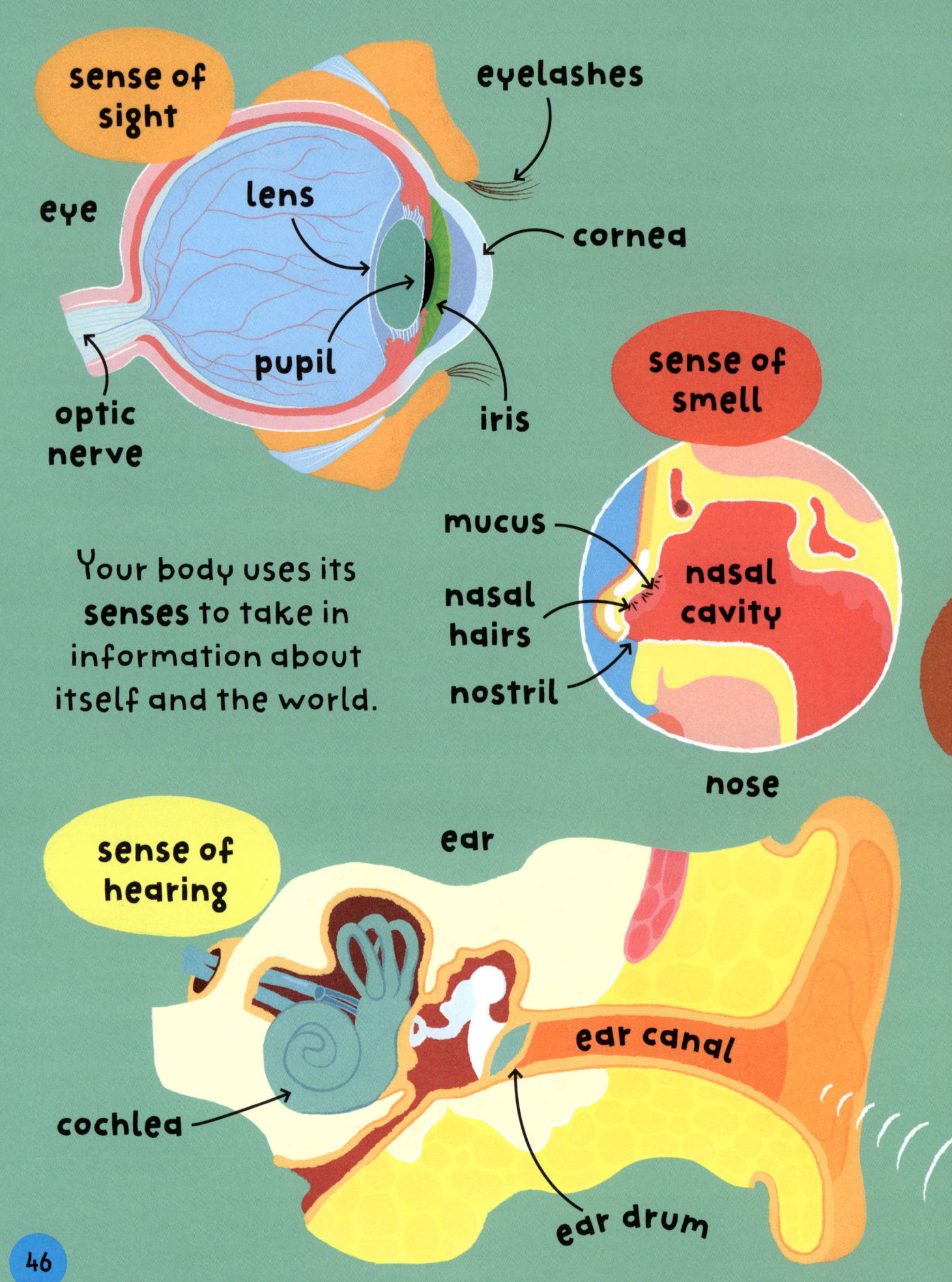

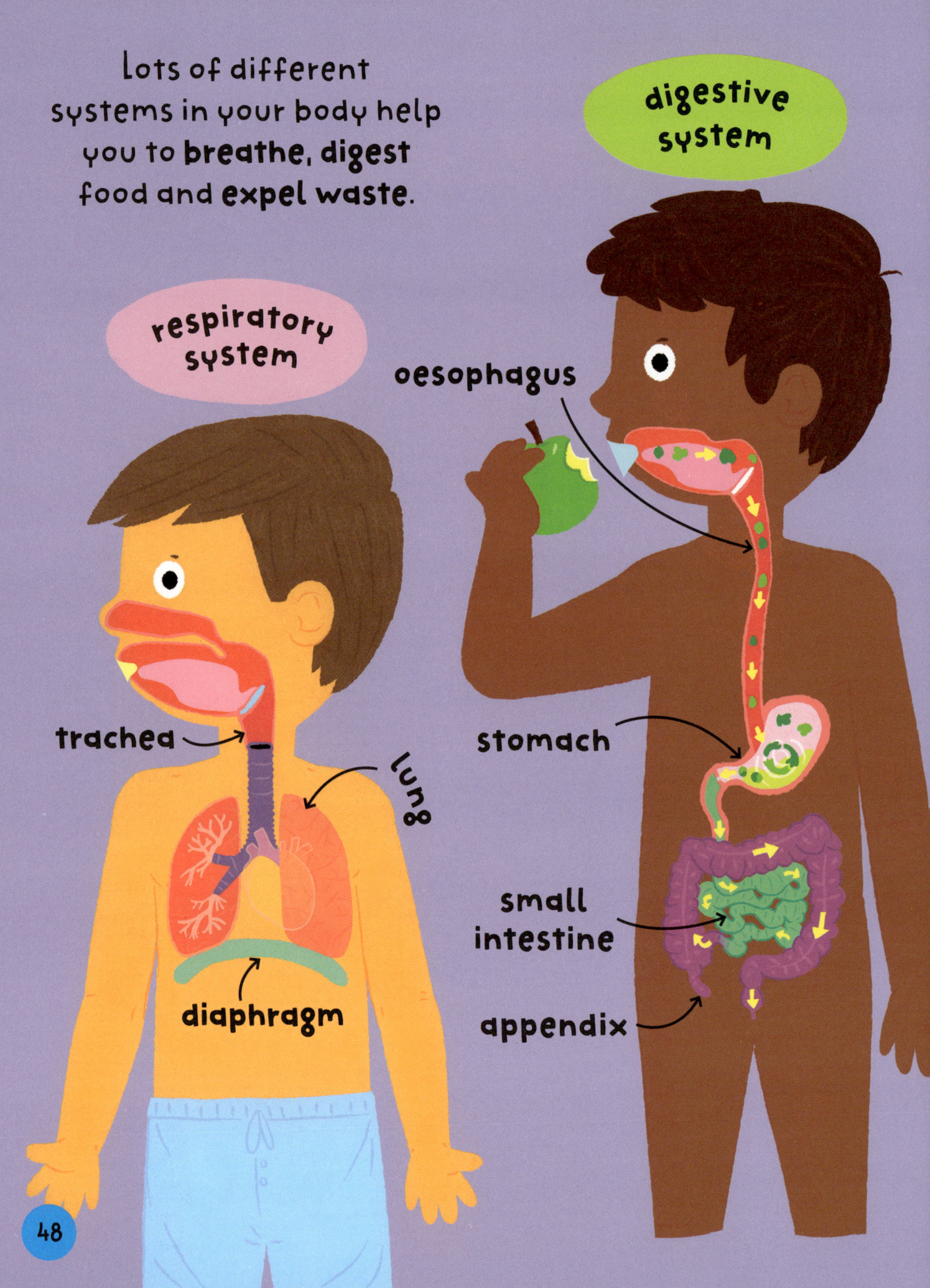

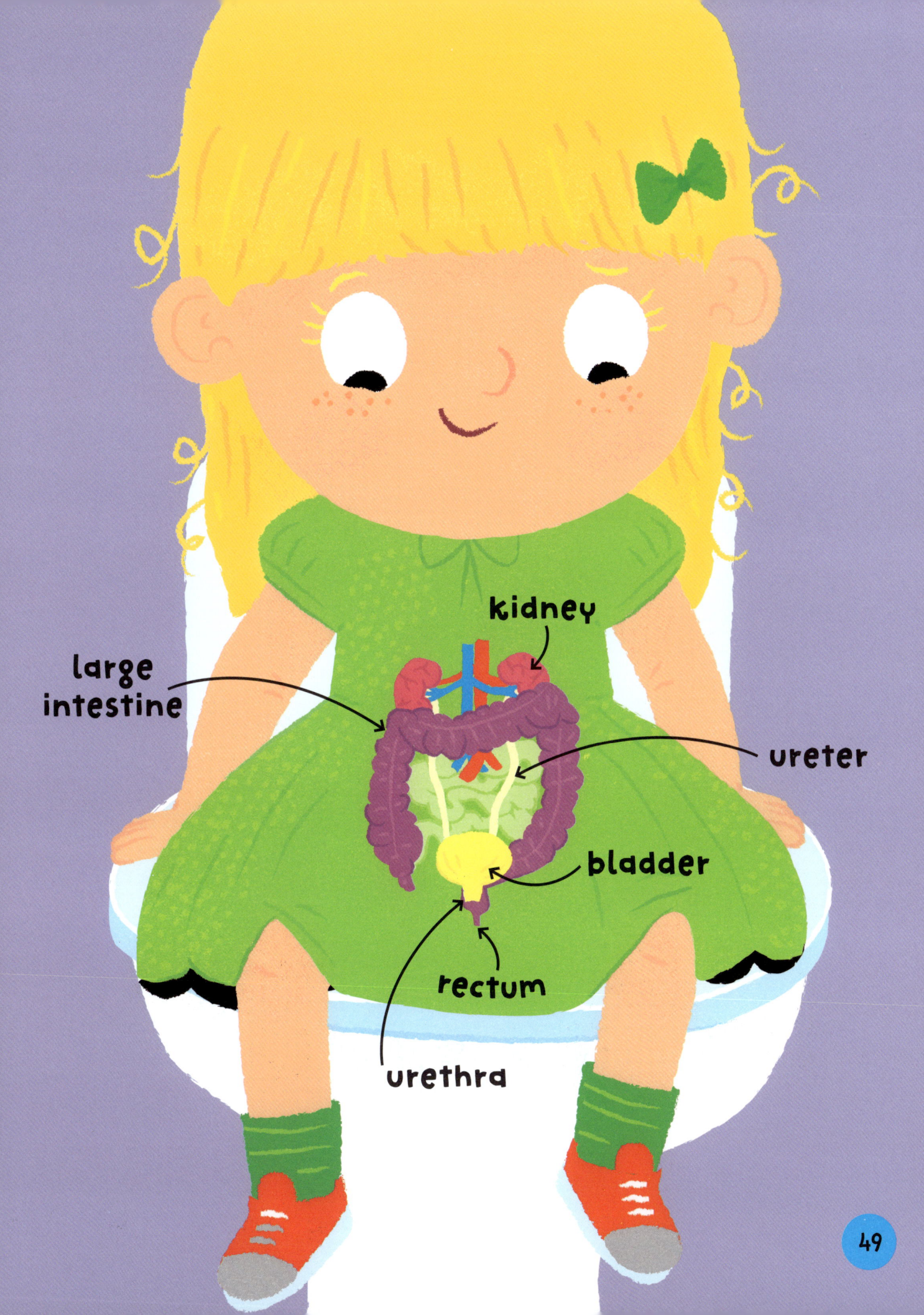

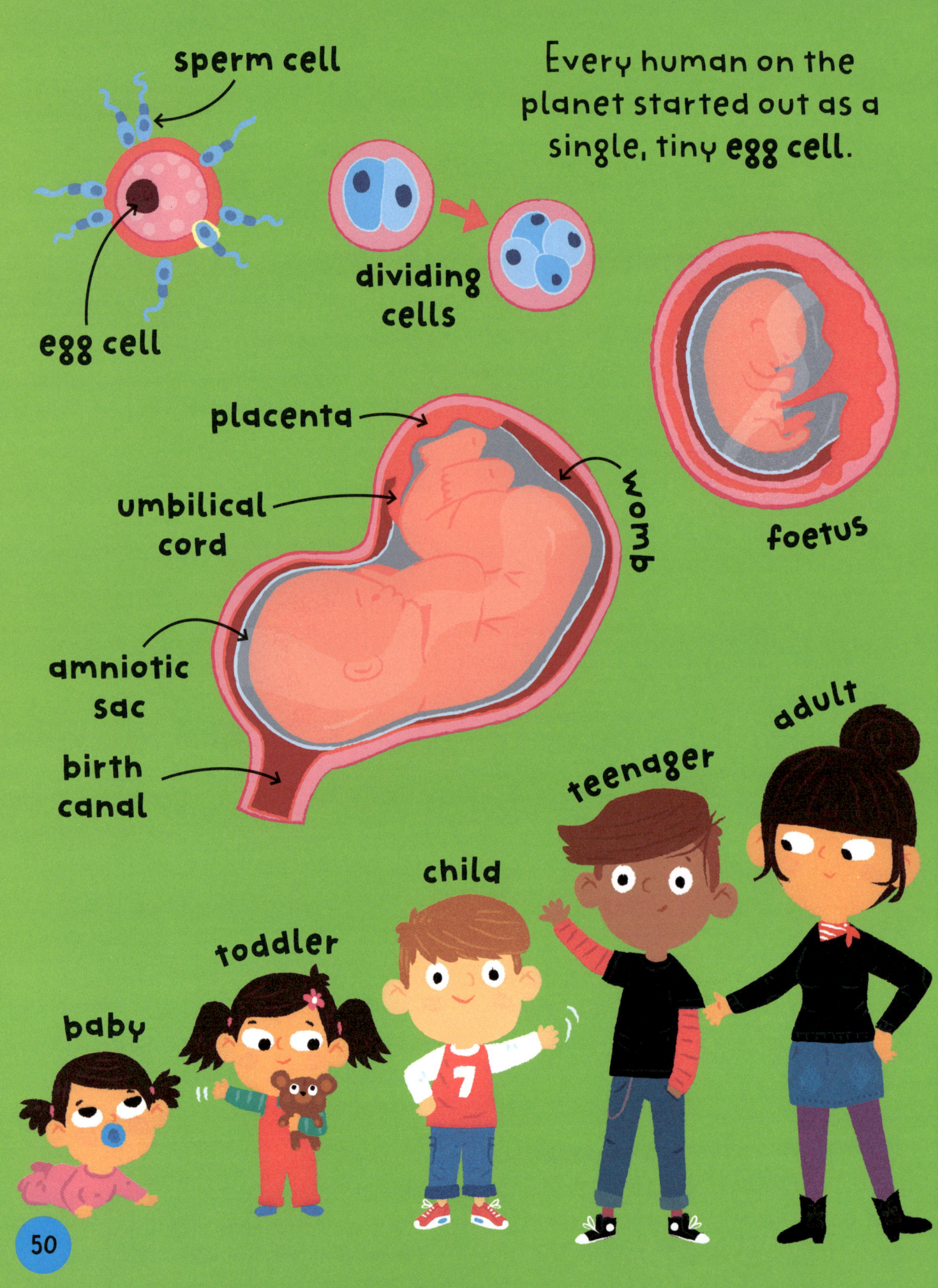

Habitats

polar

mountains

A **habitat** is a home where animals or plants can find food, water and shelter.

reindeer

pufferfish

turtle

seahorse

coral

52

gull

bottlenose dolphins

cormorant

There's lots to explore on the changing **shore**.

limpet

seaweed

crab

rockpool

starfish

A **woodland** can have thousands of trees growing in it. Every single one of them is a habitat for lots of living things.

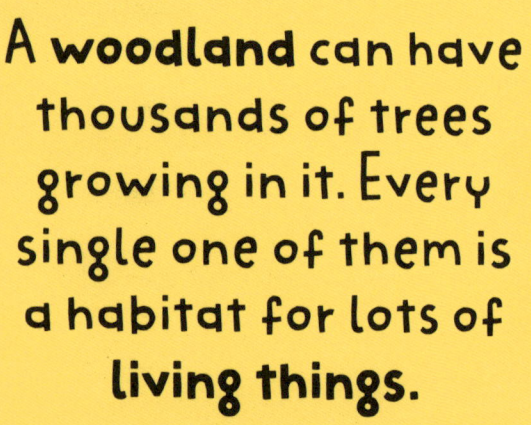
monarch butterflies

toadstools

hedgehog

foxgloves

grey squirrel

pitcher plant

leafcutter ants

All the animals and plants in a rainforest need each other to survive. This is called an **ecosystem**.

cassowary

orange-winged Amazon parrot

bird-eating tarantula

lonomia caterpillar

arctic tern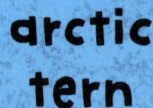

walrus

sea otters

NORTH AMERICA

puffin

Atlantic Ocean

Mid-Atlantic Ridge

manatee

Equator

Pacific Ocean

SOUTH AMERICA

great white shark

Southern Ocean

The **Pacific Ocean** is the biggest and deepest of the five oceans. The Arctic Ocean is the smallest.

Oceans near the **Equator** are warm and teeming with life. The Arctic and Southern oceans are much colder.

staghorn coral

mushroom coral

coral reef

leafy seadragon

tube coral

cuttlefish

brain coral

decorator crab

Earth

gravitational pull

high tide

Moon

low tide

wave

crest

trough

spume

The oceans are constantly moving. Wind on the surface causes waves, and the Moon creates **tides**.

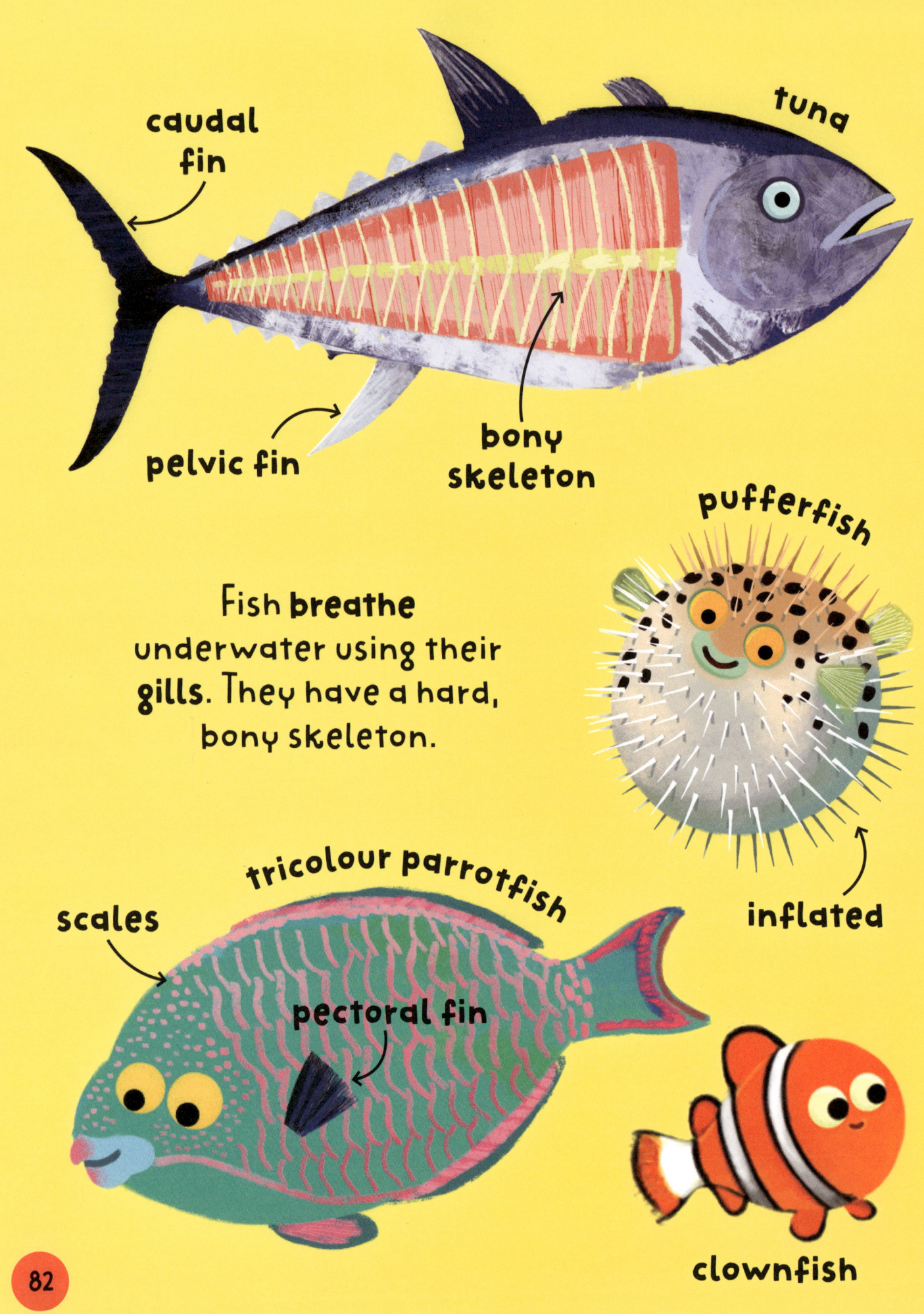

Animals

Mammals are warm-blooded and most of them give birth to live young.

bat

echolocation

lion

mountain gorilla

fur

rabbit

feeding on milk

large ears

koala

fennec fox

Many mammals **sleep** in the day and come out at **night**. They are **nocturnal**.

eucalyptus tree

European badger

sett

aardvark

carapace

turtle

sticky tongue

Reptiles are ectothermic – they are cold-blooded and rely on heat in their environment to keep them warm.

eggs

hatchling

crocodile

scales

dragonfly

compound eyes

Most animals are **vertebrates** and have a **backbone**. **Invertebrates**, like insects, have no bones.

thorax
bee
abdomen

dung beetle
exoskeleton

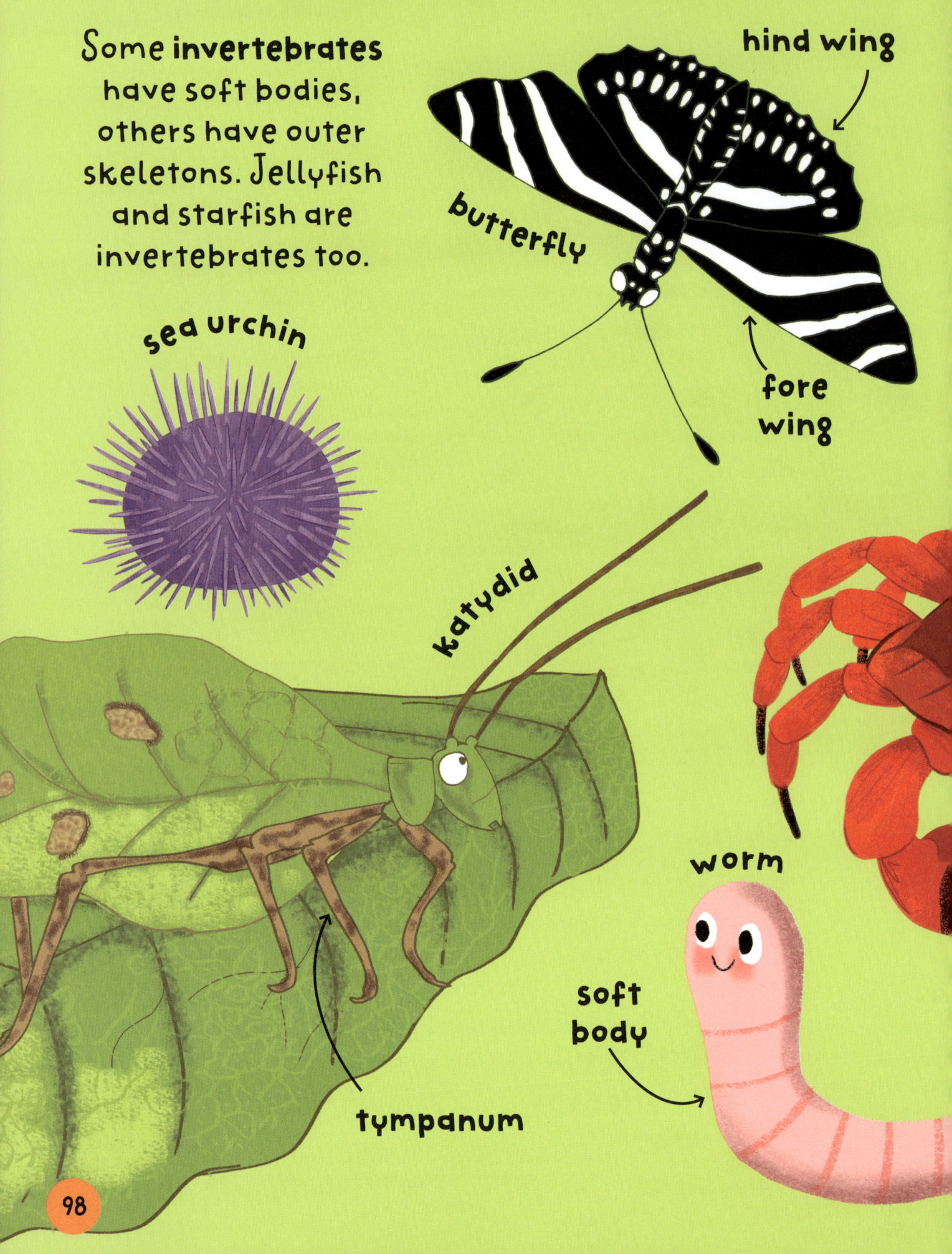

Birds

boobook owls

Birds come in all shapes, sizes and colours. They live all over the world.

birds of prey

scarlet ibis

southern crowned pigeon

crest

white goose

goslings

chick

hatching

egg shell

Farmyard birds **peck** at their food on the ground. They lay eggs and look after their chicks.

mallard ducks

male

female

Bugs

Bugs come in all shapes and sizes. Some can fly, some can jump and some can crawl.

cockchafer beetle

camouflage

leaf insect

Madagascan moon moth

arachnid

hornet

eight legs

tarantula

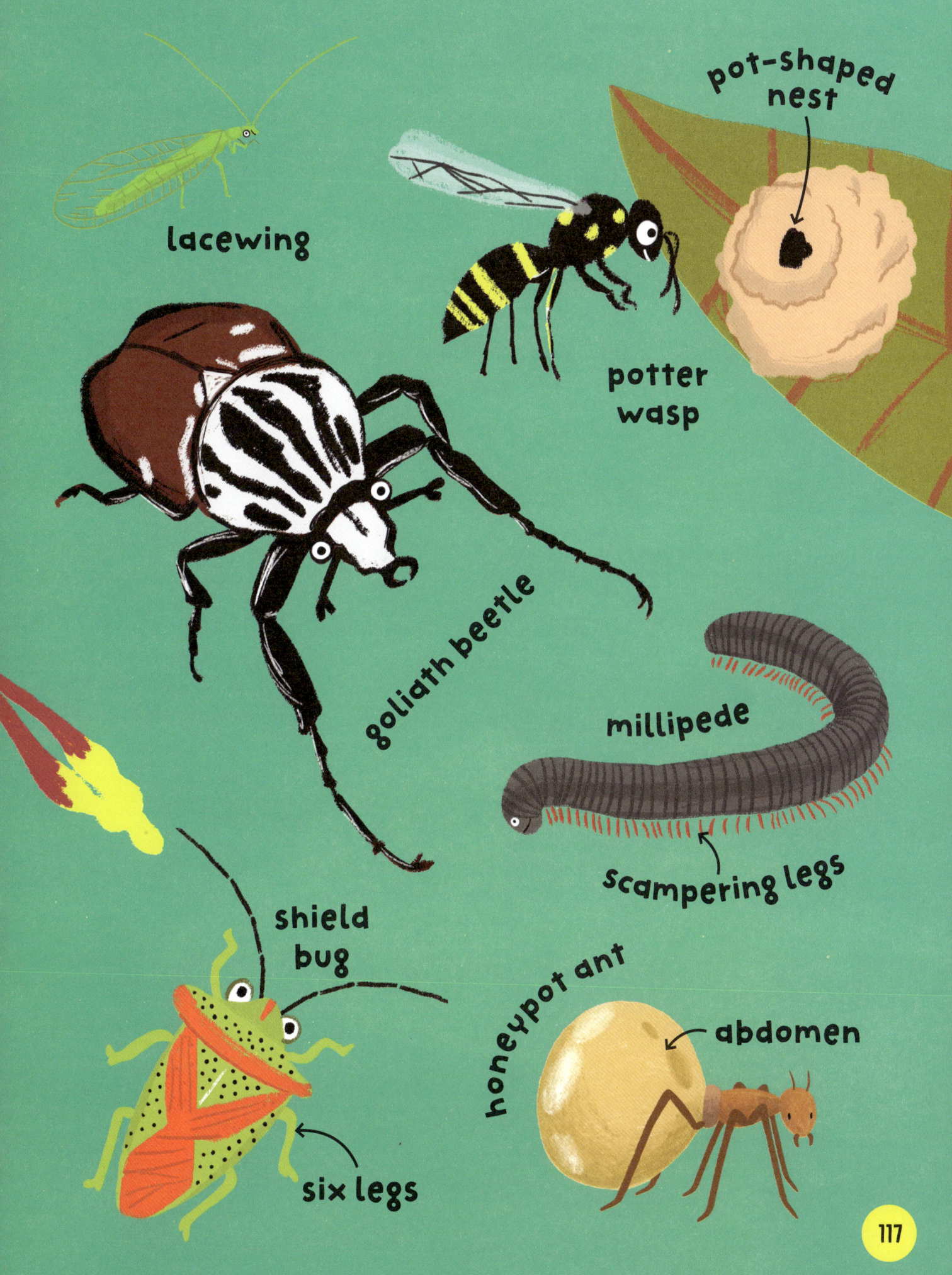

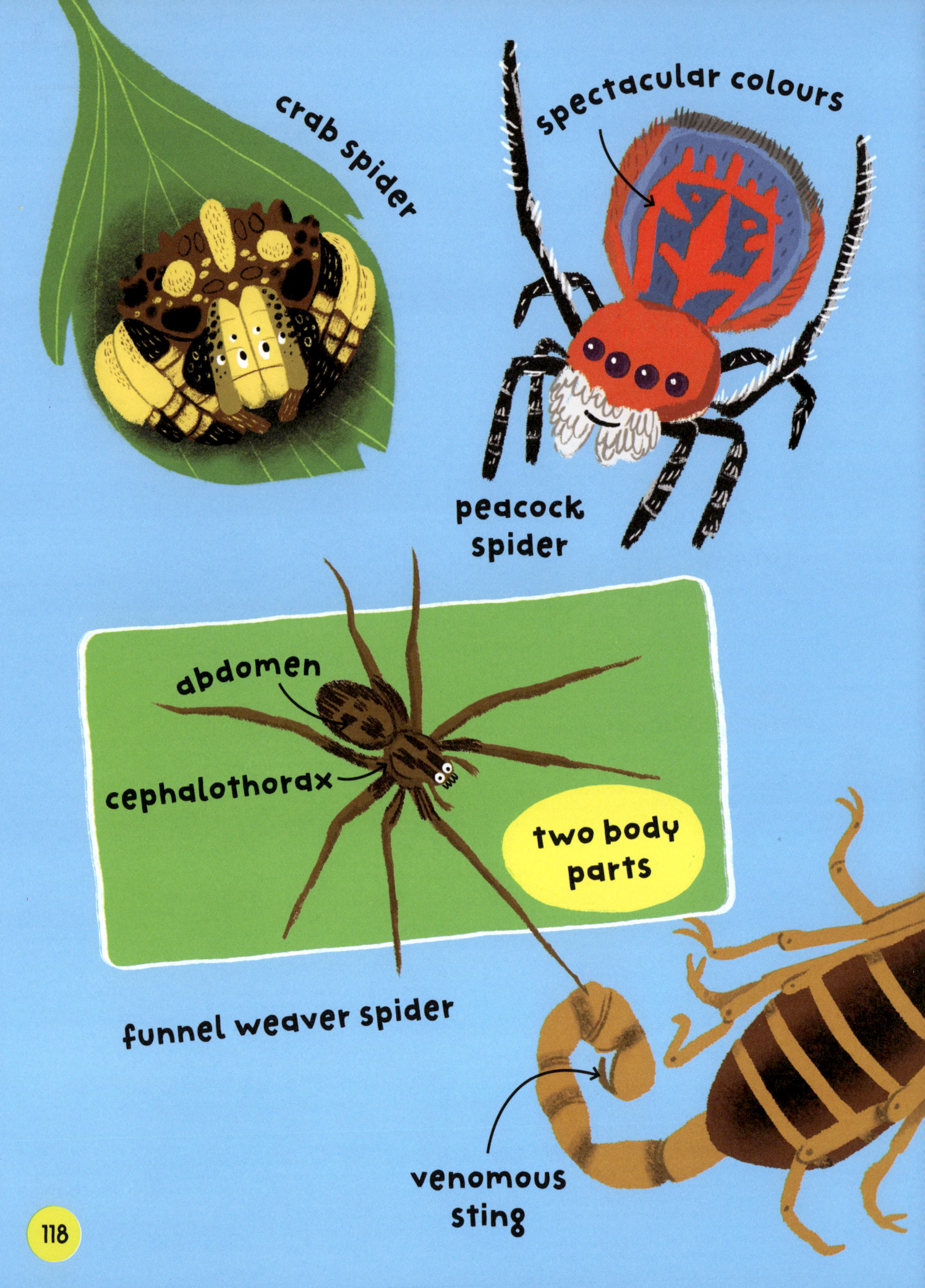

Many bugs **pollinate** plants so the plants can make seeds, and new plants will grow.

golden-brown exoskeleton

cactus bee

cactus flower

pollen wasp

clubbed antennae

stripy body

thick-legged flower beetles

petals

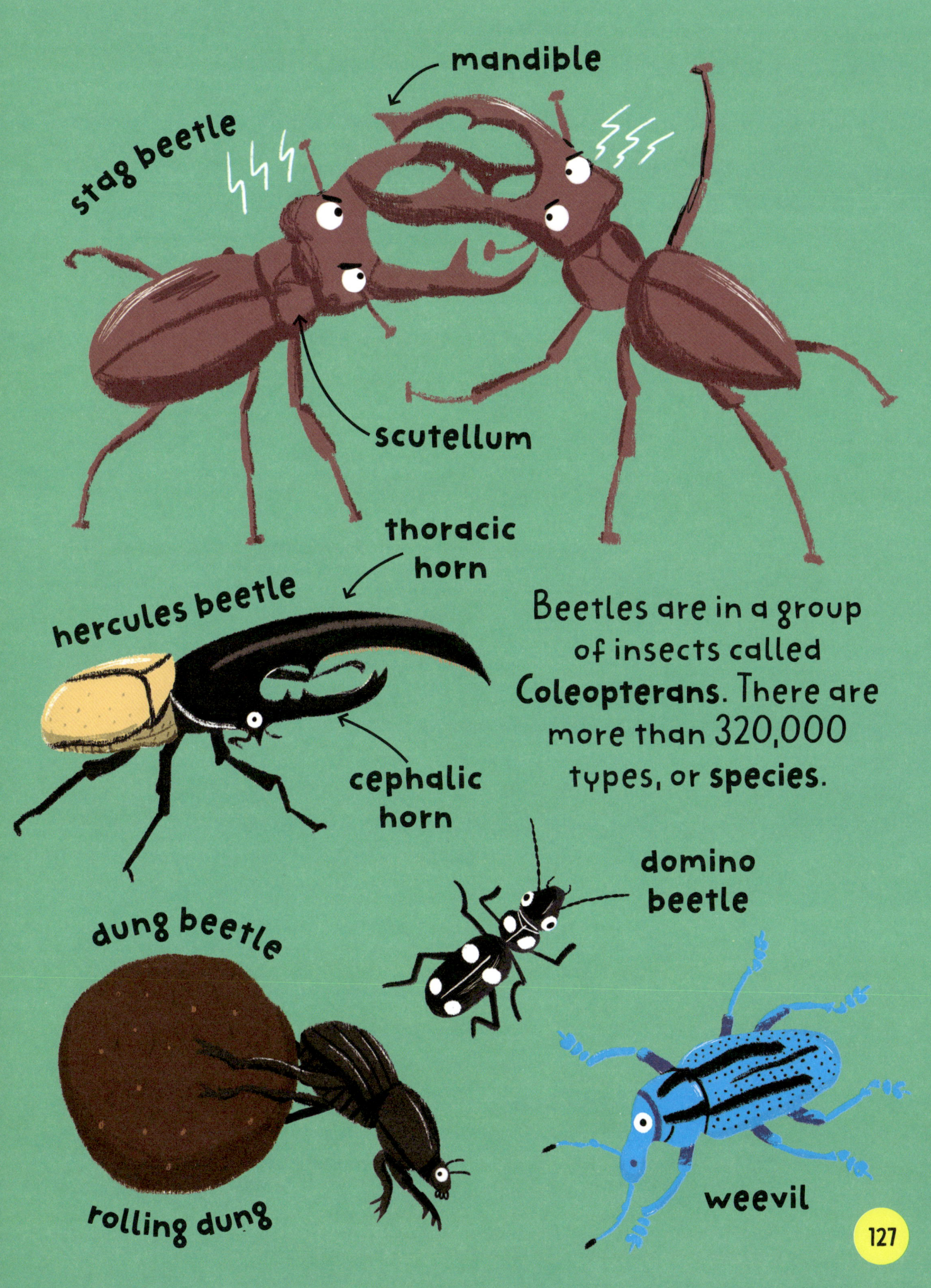

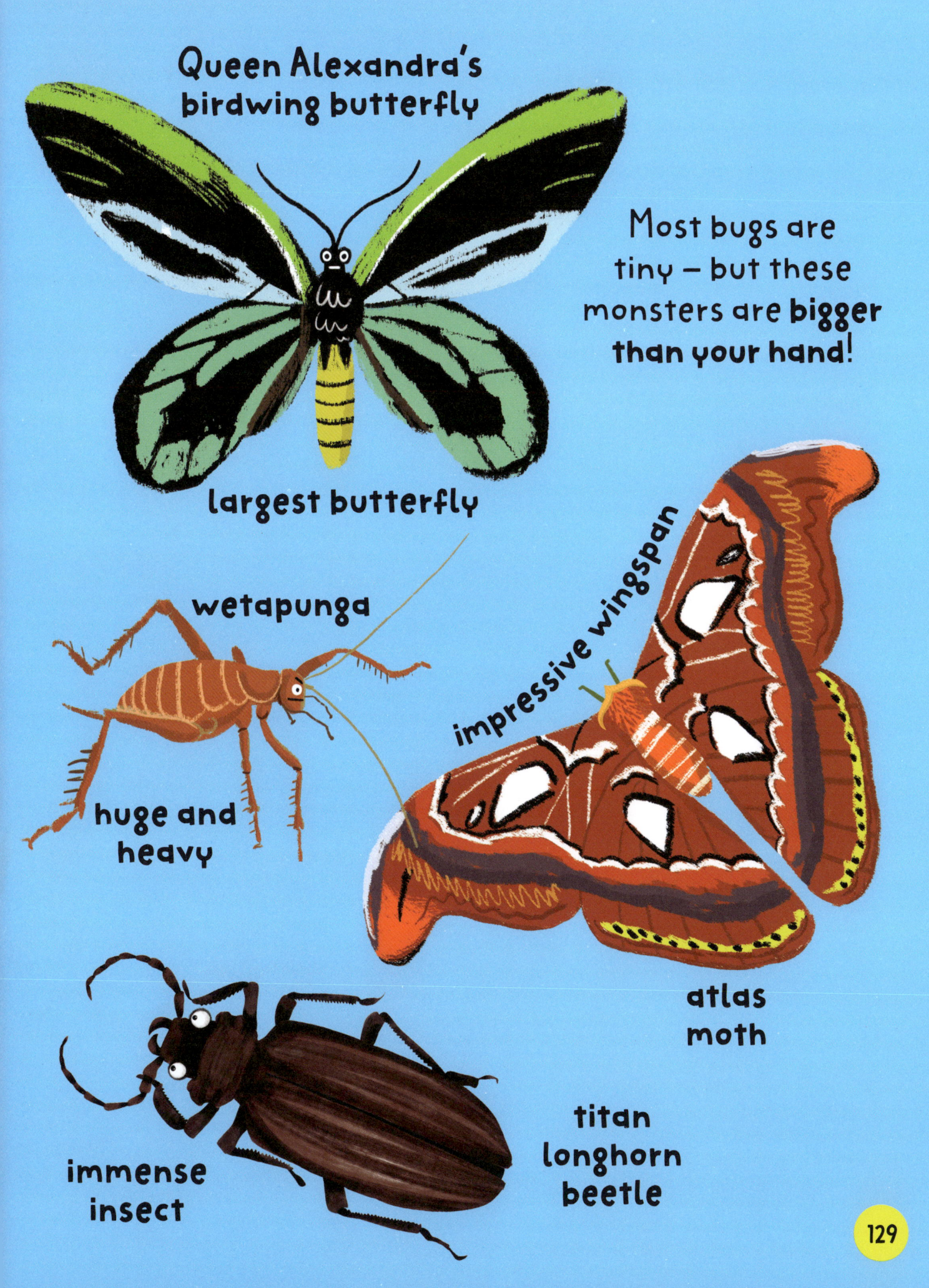

Dinosaurs

Caudipteryx

razor-sharp teeth

feathers

Allosaurus

curved teeth

Dinosaurs were **reptiles** that lived millions of years ago.

neural spine sail

Spinosaurus

Dinosaurs came in all **shapes** and **sizes** with spikes, crests and claws.

Deinonychus

Parasaurolophus

curved claw

Fossils take thousands and sometimes millions of years to form.

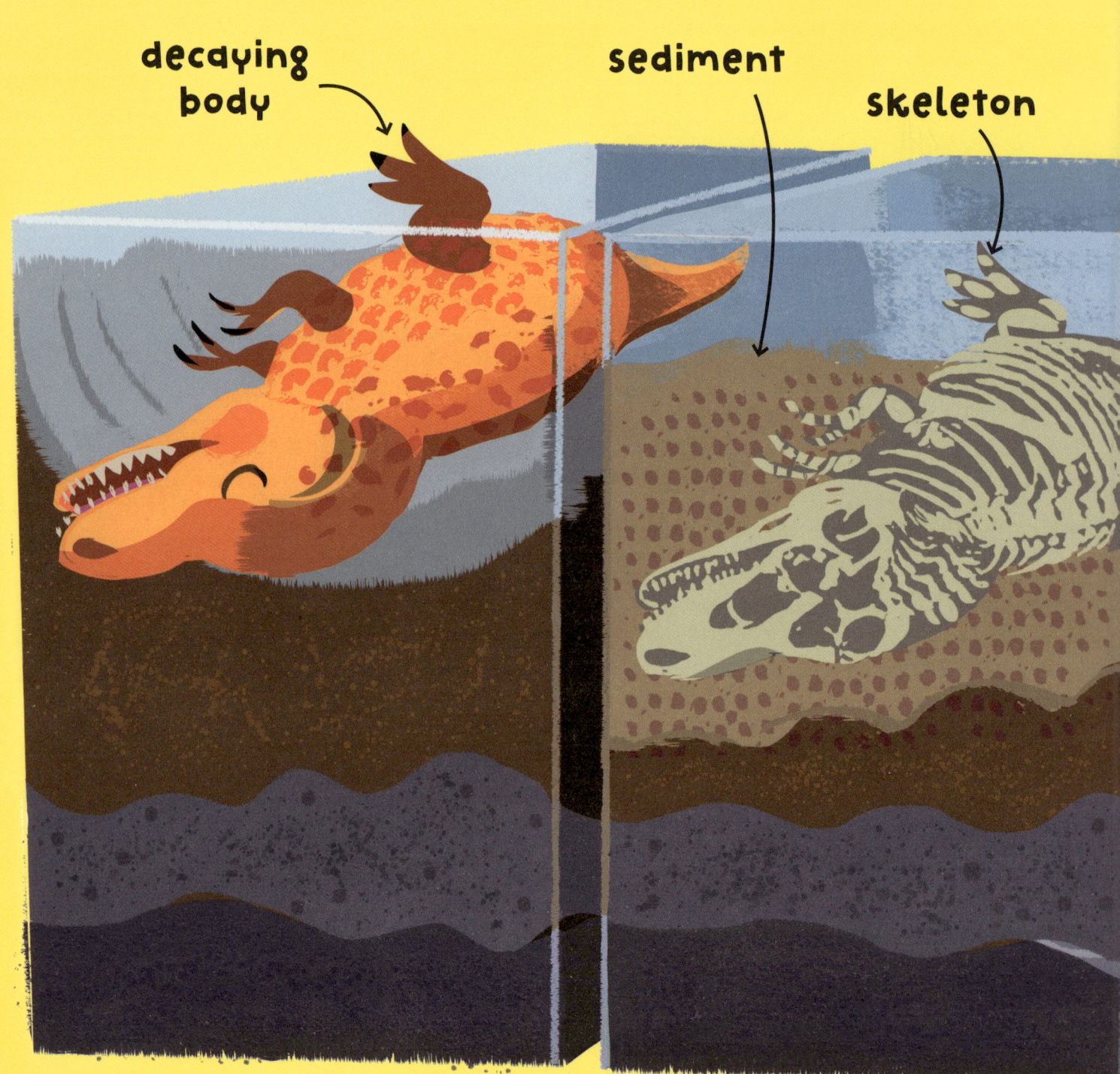

decaying body

sediment

skeleton

How to **pronounce** the names (as they appear in the book):

Caudipteryx	caw-DIP-ter-iks
Allosaurus	AL-oh-SORE-us
Tyrannosaurus rex	tie-RAN-oh-sore-us rex
Coelopysis	see-loh-FIE-sis
Eoraptor	EE-oh-RAP-tor
Compsognathus	komp-sog-NATH-us
Gallimimus	gal-lee-MY-mus
Albertosaurus	AL-bert-oh-SORE-us
Apatosaurus	a-PAT-oh-sore-us
Stegosaurus	STEG-oh-SORE-us
Nigersaurus	nai-ja-SORE-us
Triceratops	tri-SERRA-tops
Nyctosaurus	NIC-to-SORE-us
Pteranodon	te-RAN-oh-don
Quetzalcoatlus	ket-zal-KWAT-luss
Nemicolopterus	NEM-ee-kol-OPT-er-us
Liopleurodon	LIE-oh-PLUR-a-don
Mosasaurus	moe-za-SORE-us
Ophthalmosaurus	op-THAL-mo-SORE-us
Elasmosaurus	el-lazz-mo-SORE-us
Microraptor	MY-crow-RAP-tor
Iguanodon	ig-WHA-noh-don
Therizinosaurus	thera-ZINA-SORE-us
Parasaurolophus	para-sore-ROL-oh-fus
Spinosaurus	SPY-noh-SORE-us
Deinonychus	di-NON-ee-kus
Velociraptor	ve-LOSS-ee-RAP-tor
Diplodocus	DIP-lo-DOKE-us
Ankylosaurus	an-KIE-lo-sore-us
Troodon	TRUE-oh-don
Maiasaura	my-a-SORE-a